A, B, C's

The American Indian Way

by Richard Red Hawk

Sierra Oaks Publishing Company
1988

Other Children's Books By Sierra Oaks Publishing Company:

Grandmother's Christmas Story: A True Quechan Indian Story
A Trip to a Pow Wow
Grandmother Stories of the Northwest
Grandfather's Story of Navajo Monsters
Grandfather's Origin Story: The Navajo Indian Beginning

Copyright © 1988

Sierra Oaks Publishing Company
P.O. Box 255354
Sacramento, California   95658-5354

ISBN: 0-940113-15-5

For Indian children everywhere and
for all children who want to know more
about American Indians

ACKNOWLEDGEMENTS

Special thanks is extended to the Title IV, Indian Education Program teachers and to the many elementary school teachers who encouraged me to do this project. I also thank the following people and institutions for sharing the photographs used in this book.

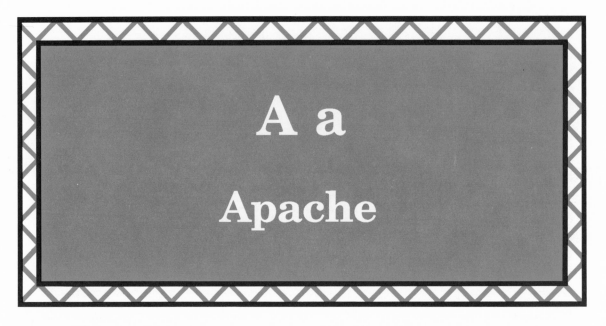

A a

Apache

Apache Indians live mostly in the southwestern part of the United States. There are many different bands of Apaches. This is a picture of Geronimo. He was a famous Apache war chief. In 1886, he stopped fighting. The army sent Geronimo and his Apache band away from Arizona. He was never allowed to return to the Southwest.

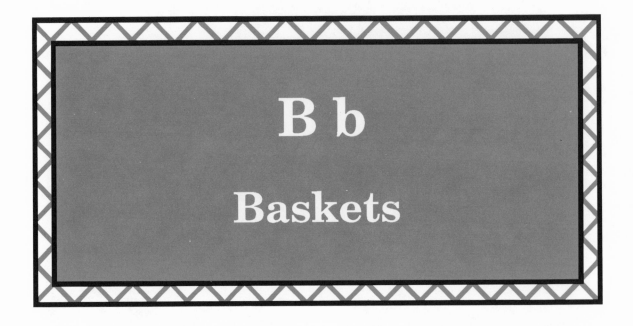

B b
Baskets

Baskets were used by Indians to store food and water. Some Indians cooked in baskets. Indians make many kinds of baskets. Here an Indian from southern California is weaving a star pattern into a rare basket.

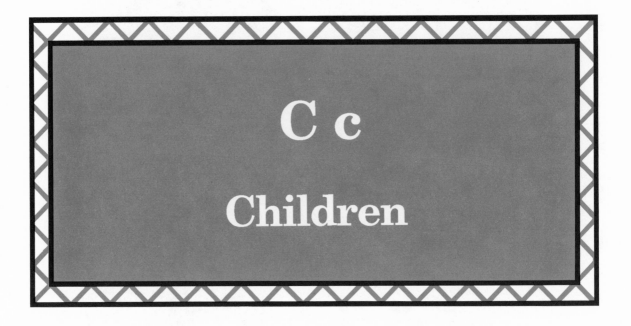

C c

Children

Children are very important to American Indians. This child is an Indian girl from the Northwest. Indians care about their families. They also care about their children. Today Indian children go to school, sing, and play like other children. They are proud to be American Indians.

6

D d
Drums

Drums are used by all Indians. The drums in this picture were used in a ceremony. Drums were used for many events. Indians also played other musical instruments. They used flutes, horns, and rattles to make music.

9

E e
Eagle feathers

Eagle feathers are special to American Indians. The feathers of eagles are used for headdresses. The Indian in this picture has a special eagle feather placed in his hair. Eagle feathers are used by Indians during special events.

11

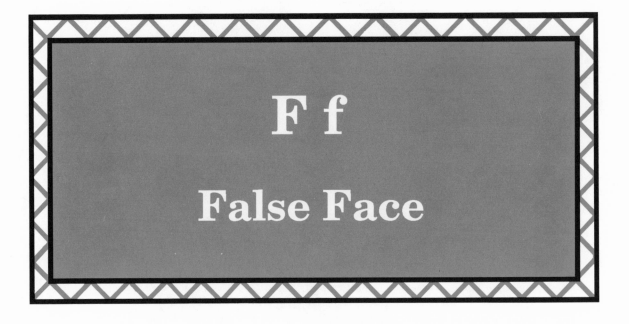

F f

False Face

False Face is a mask made by the Iroquois Indians. Senecas, Onondagas, Oneidas, Mohawks, Cayugas, and Tuscaroras are all Iroquois Indians. They make False Face masks for ceremonies. False Face masks represent special power.

12

13

G g
Gloves

Gloves are worn by many Indians. Gloves protect the hands from cold weather. Some Indians decorate their gloves. The man and two women in this picture are wearing gloves decorated with many beads. The beads are colorful. These Northwestern Indians like to decorate their gloves with flower designs.

H h

Horse

Horses are important to some American Indians today. They were very important to Indians in the past. The Spanish brought horses to America. Indians started using horses, too. They traveled and hunted on horses. Some Indians used horses to pull tipi poles and packed their belongings on horses.

16

17

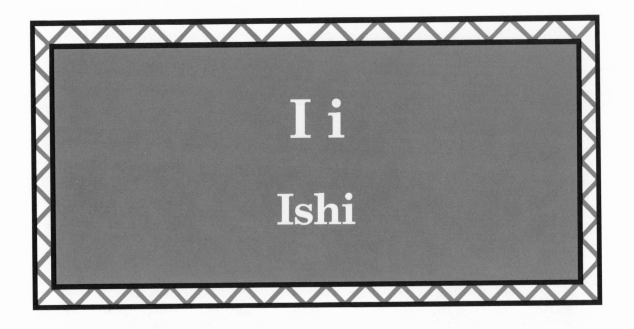

I i
Ishi

Ishi was a famous Yahi Indian of northern California. He spent the early part of his life living in the canyons, forests, and mountains. He was a kind and patient man. Ishi taught us many things about American Indian life in California.

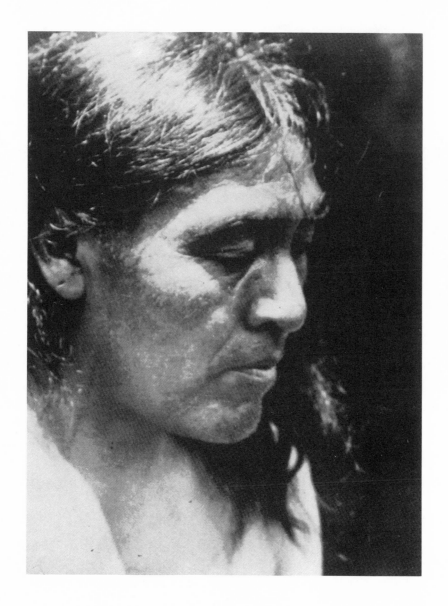

19

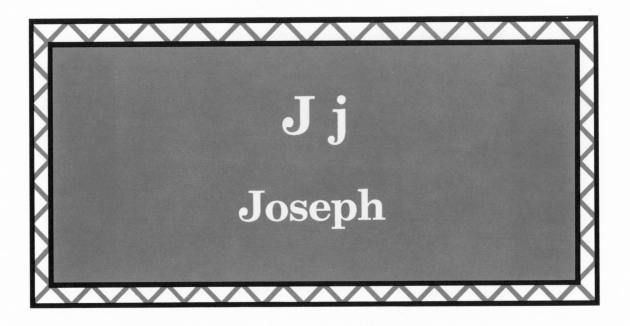

J j

Joseph

Joseph was a Nez Perce Indian. His Indian name meant Thunder Rising Over Loftier Mountain Heights. Joseph lived in Oregon on the Nez Perce Reservation. He wanted peace, but his people went to war when they lost their lands. Chief Joseph and some Nez Perce had to leave their land and live on the Colville Reservation in the state of Washington.

20

21

K k

Kachinas

Kachinas are dolls made by Hopi and Zuni Indians. These are cloud kachinas made by a Hopi Indian man named Paul Coochyamptewa. The kachina on the right is a *taka* or man. The kachina on the left is a *mana* or woman. Kachinas bring rain for the Hopis living in Arizona.

23

L l
Luiseño

Luiseño Indians live in southern California. They have lived in California for hundreds of years. This Luiseño Indian is Henry Rodriguez. He is an elder and leader of the La Jolla Indian Tribe. He is a teacher who shares stories with many children.

25

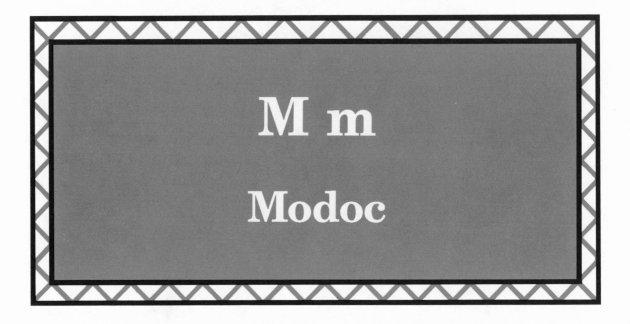

M m
Modoc

Modocs are American Indians from northern California. Today most Modocs live in Oregon and Oklahoma. This man's Modoc name was *Keintpoos*, but his nickname was Captain Jack. He became a leader of the Modocs after his people and the United States Army began to fight.

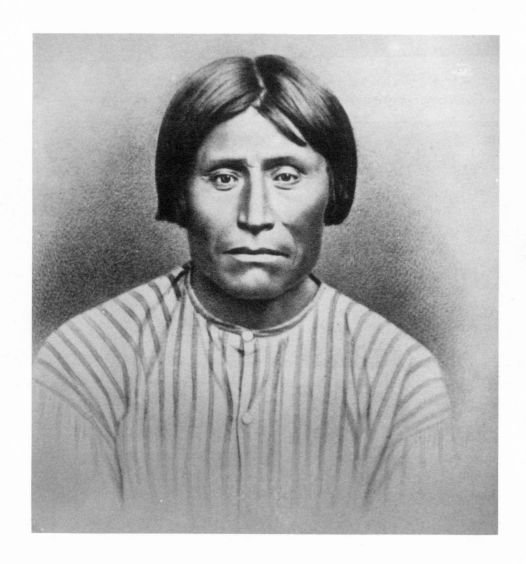

27

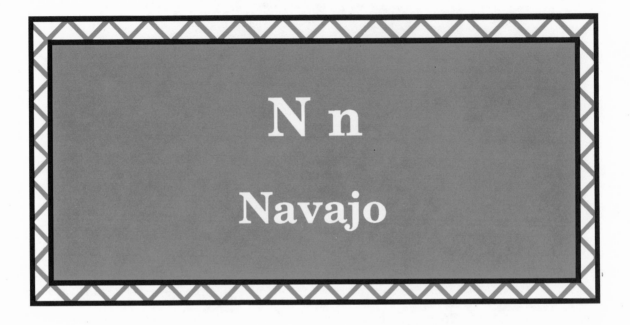

N n

Navajo

Navajo Indians live on a large reservation. Many Navajos live in Arizona, New Mexico, and Utah. The Navajos have the largest Indian Tribe in the United States. Navajos are known for their art, their music, and their ceremonies.

29

Ollokot was a Nez Perce chief. In English his name means
Frog. He was the brother of Chief Joseph. Ollokot was a war chief.
He led the young warriors during the Nez Perce War of 1877.

31

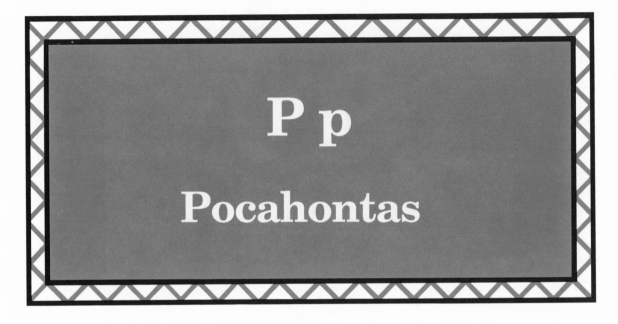

P p
Pocahontas

Pocahontas was a Pamunkey Indian. She was the daughter of Chief Powhatan. Pocahontas became a friend of the English settlers at Jamestown, Virginia. She helped the English and married an Englishman named John Rolfe. Pocahontas wanted the Indians and the English to be friends.

Ætatis suæ 21. Aº. 1616.

33

Q q
Quechan

Quechan Indians live in the southeastern corner of California. They live along the banks of the Colorado River. Quechan women farmed the lands along the river. They also made beautiful capes out of beads. The beaded capes are made from red and white or blue and white beads.

35

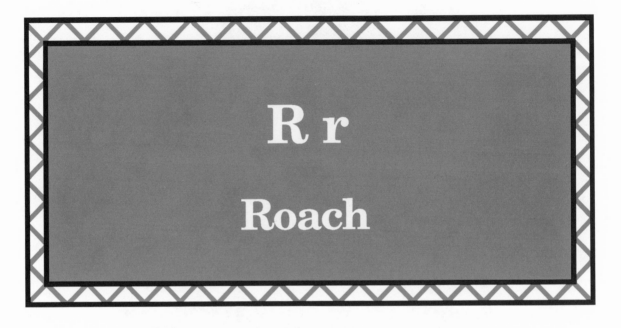

R r
Roach

Roaches are a type of headdress. American Indians from many parts of the country wear roaches. Roaches are made from the hair of the porcupine. The hair is sewn into white-tail deer hide. Sometimes Indians put eagle feathers in the middle of the roach.

37

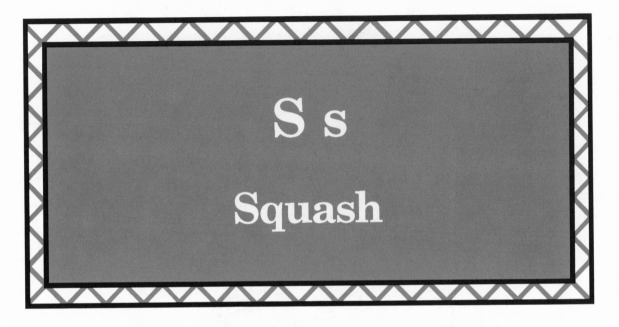

S s

Squash

Squash is a food grown by American Indians. It is a special food for many Indians. Squash, corn, beans, potatoes, and tomatoes are all American Indian foods grown by Indian farmers. This picture shows a Squash Kachina of the Hopi Indians.

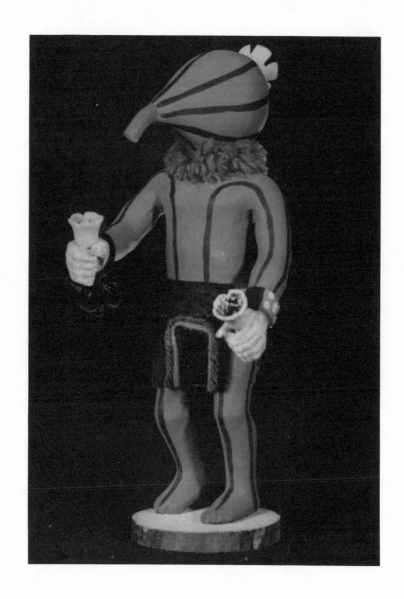

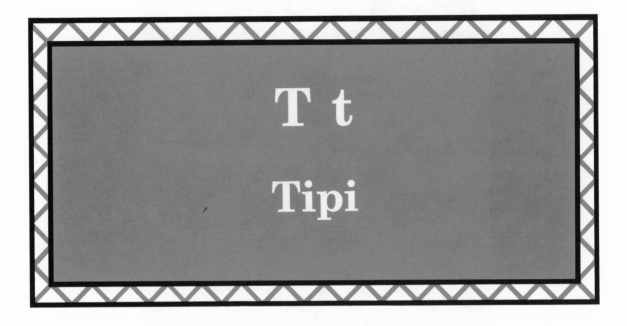

T t

Tipi

A tipi is one kind of American Indian home. Indians who lived on the Great Plains lived in tipis. The Sioux, Cheyenne, and Comanche tribes all used tipis for their houses. Other Indians lived in tipis, too. Tipis were made out of buffalo hide. Modern tipis like this one are made out of canvas.

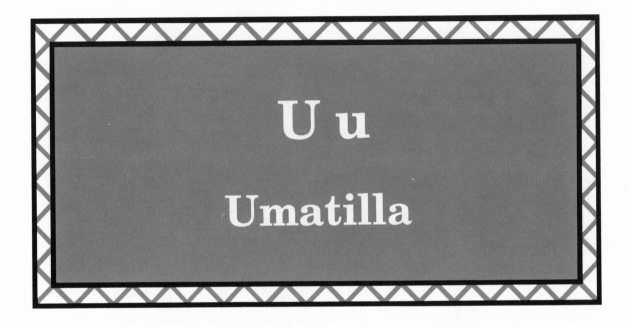

U u

Umatilla

Umatilla Indians live in the Northwest. William Charley was a Umatilla Indian from Oregon. He is wearing a headdress made from a roach and a line of eagle feathers. Bear claws are placed in the crown of his roach. Bears, eagles, and porcupines are important animals to the Umatillas.

43

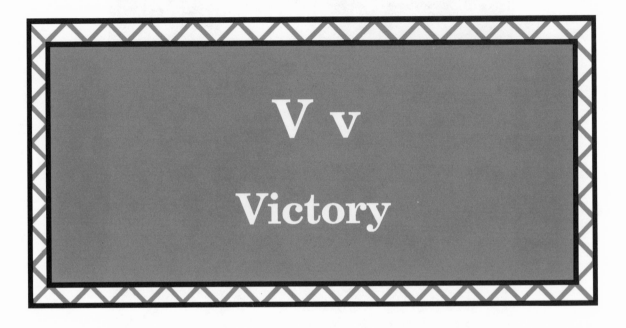

Victory was important to American Indians. Girls and boys were taught to seek victories. They were also taught cooperation. When girls and boys were victorious in their work and duties, people celebrated. Delores George won a victory in 1958 when she was named Queen of the Pow Wow on the Yakima Reservation.

45

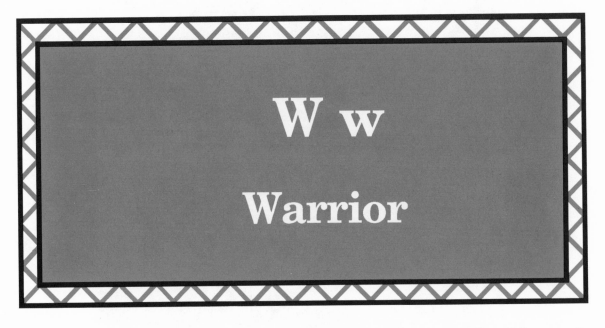

W w

Warrior

Warriors were people who fought for their people. Men and women could be warriors. Even boys and girls fought as warriors. When Yellow Wolf was a boy, he became a warrior. Some Indians believe that they are warriors today whenever they help Indian people. Warriors protect and encourage others to do well and to do each other no harm.

47

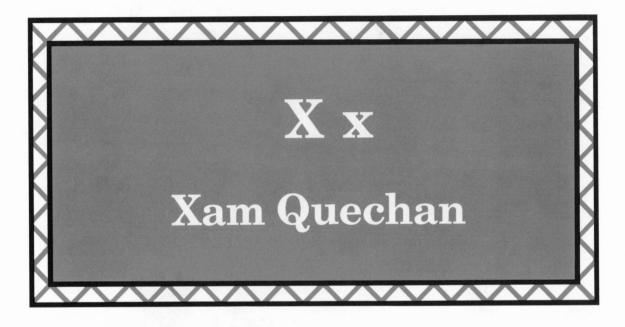

X x

Xam Quechan

Xam Quechan describes a special trail taken by one tribe of Indians in southern California. The trail followed by the Quechan Indians was a good road. It led them down off a mountain and to the rich farmlands along the Colorado River. This baby, mother, and father knew the happiness of Xam Quechan.

49

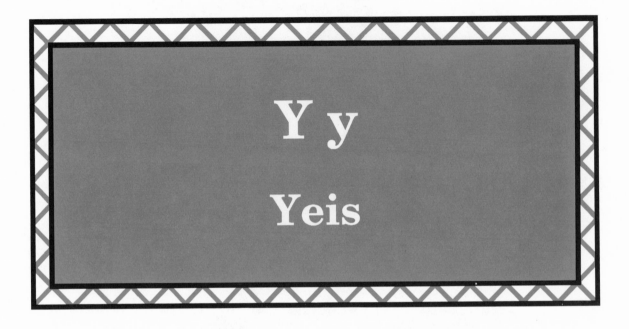

Yy

Yeis

Yeis are Navajo Indian spirits. Navajos believe that yeis have the power to cure illness. During some ceremonies men and women wear yei masks. The masks are brightly painted. When they are old enough, girls and boys are initiated. They learn all about the yeis when they are initiated.

50

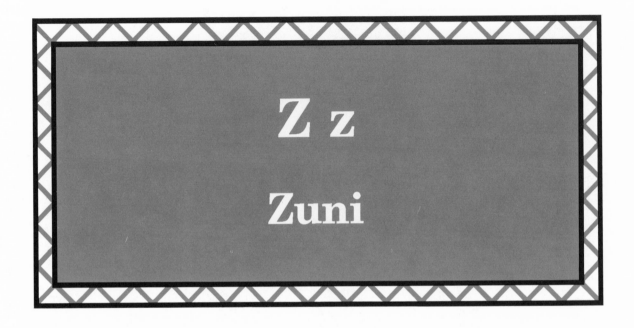

Z z

Zuni

Zuni is an Indian pueblo or town. It is located in New Mexico. The Indians living at the pueblo are called Zunis. The Zunis are well known for their beautiful art. They make colorful jewelry out of turquoise, coral, and white shell. Zunis also make white pottery with black and red figures painted on it.

53

PHOTOGRAPH CREDITS

A   Geronimo, Bureau of American Ethnology, Smithsonian Institution

B   Quechan Basketmaker, Yuma County Historical Society

C   Yakima Child, Yakima Valley Regional Library

D   Drum, Yakima Valley Regional Library

E   Harlish Washomake, Bureau of American Ethnology, Smithsonian Institution

F   False Face Mask, Author's Photo, San Diego Museum of Man

G   Gloves, Yakima Valley Regional Library

H   Horses, Yakima Valley Regional Library

I   Ishi, Lowie Museum

J   Joseph, Washington State University Library

K   Kachinas, Author's Photo by Dennis Coleman

L   Luiseño, Author's Photo by Mariska and Ramona Emry

M	Modoc, Bureau of American Ethnology, Smithsonian Institution
N	Navajo, Bureau of American Ethnology, Smithsonian Institution
O	Ollokot, Washington State University Library
P	Pocahontas, National Portrait Gallery, Smithsonian Institution
Q	Quechan, Yuma County Historical Society
R	Roach, Oregon Historical Society
S	Squash Kachina, Author's Photo by Dennis Coleman
T	Tipi, Yakima Valley Regional Library
U	Umatilla, Oregon Historical Society
V	Victory, Yakima Valley Regional Library
W	Warrior, Washington State University Library
X	Xam Quechan, Yuma County Historical Society
Y	Yei, Author's Photo, San Diego Museum of Man
Z	Zuni, National Archives by Richard H. Kern